THE PURPOSE OF LIFE

Dedication

Firstly, I dedicate this book to God, the One who has given me the ability and wisdom to write this book for his glory only.

I recognize that I am only the instrument God was pleased to use to bring this project, which originated in his heart, into the world. To the One who sent his Son to die on the cross for our sins, to him alone be the glory.

Secondly, I want to thank my husband. He is one of the reasons why I didn't give up on the process of the book, always believing in the gift God placed in me, always encouraging me to keep going, and always checking up on me if I had made any progress. Without his help and encouragement, I wouldn't have made it.

I also want to thank my pastor who took the time to help me with the book.

THE PURPOSE OF LIFE

Discover God's Plan For You

Advantage
BOOKS

Monica Rosario Santos

Library of Congress Catalog Number: APPLIED FOR

Name: Rosario Santos, Monica, Author
Title: ***The Purpose of Life***
Monica Rosario Santos
Advantage Books, 2023
Identifiers: ISBN Paperback: 978159756866
Subjects:

First Printing: August 2023

23 24 25 26 27 28   10 9 8 7 6 5 4 3 2 1

Table of Contents

DEDICATION 2

1: HOW IT ALL BEGAN 7

2: THE MYSTERY OF GOD 13

3: THE NECESSITY OF HAVING CHRIST 17

4: WHAT HINDERS PEOPLE FROM COMING TO CHRIST 25

5: IF I BECOME A CHRISTIAN DOES IT MEAN I WON'T SIN ANYMORE? . 39

6: SPIRITUAL BLINDNESS 43

7: GOD'S WARNINGS 51

8: CONSEQUENCES OF A LIFE SEPARATED FROM CHRIST 58

9: REPENTANCE 76

1

HOW IT ALL BEGAN

I was once in school; we were having our lunch break and my friends were discussing various topics. Suddenly, one of them said, "what's the purpose of life if we all die anyway?."

The first thing I thought when I listened to that, is that without Christ there is no purpose to life because technically we live to die at the end.

What not everyone knows or instead chooses to ignore is that there is something beyond death, in fact, your life now will determine your eternal future and is that future that brings meaning to our actual existence and the one that truly matters.

We were created (Genesis 1:26-28) to live in communion with God, but when Adam and Eve introduced sin (by disobeying God's command) and consequently death, humanity was separated from God (Romans 3:23).

This event opened the door for the devil to cause us to stumble having, therefore, influence over our lives and consequently leading us to hell along with him because of our disobedience to God.

From that moment sin dwelt within us, and our hearts were filled with wickedness.

This wickedness resulted in the first crime committed by Cain, Abel's brother. Both were Adam and Eve's sons, but Abel was righteous in God's eyes because of his good deeds, which came from a heart which desired to please God (his deeds were a consequent act of his willingness to please God, not the reason for his righteousness).

Wickedness continued to increase to the extent in which God warned Noah, a righteous man (Genesis 6:9), to build an ark because He was going to send judgement upon the earth for the wickedness dwelling within mankind's heart.

Later on, God called a man, Abraham, telling him to leave where he lived and begin the journey into a land that God would show him, the promised land, Canaan. He promised Abraham that He would make him into a great nation, even though his wife was infertile, through which God will bless all nations (Galatians 3:8).

This promise concerns the physical and spiritual realms. Abraham had a son called Ismael, with Sarah's slave called Hagar (Genesis 16:1-4). He then had a second son, the son of the promise (Genesis 15:4), Isaac, with his wife Sarah.

Four hundred years later God spoke to Moses (Exodus 2 and 3) and told him to bring his people out of Egypt, where the Israelites were in slavery. With great power, God delivered his people from slavery (Exodus 7-12).

The Israelites were guided by God through the desert (their time was extended to 40 years due to their disobedience) toward the promised land. During this period of time, God gave Moses the Law, which means that the Israelites were under the law. According to Galatians 3:19, the purpose of the Law was to show us the sinful nature within us and directs us toward Christ:

Galatians 3:19 EXB "So what was the law for? It was given to show that the wrong things people do are against God's will. And it continued until the special descendant, who had been promised, came."

However, salvation is not based on our obedience to the law (by works; Ephesians 2:8) because Galatians 3:10-11 says,

Galatians 3:10-11 NIV "For all who rely on the works of the law are under curse, as it is written; Cursed is everyone who does not continue to do everything written in the Book

of the Law. Clearly, no one who relies on the law is justified before God, because the righteous will live by faith."

These two women, Hagar and Sarah, represent the two covenants of God. Hagar, the slave, represents Mount Sinai where the Law was given. Those born under this covenant were subject to slavery to their sinfulness as the Law reveals our sin, yet has no way to provide freedom from it. Sarah represents the covenant under which we can obtain freedom from sin, as she is the free woman.

Christ came to break the bondage of sin in which those born under the first covenant lived by;

Galatians 4:1-7 NLT "Think of it this way. If a father dies and leaves an inheritance for his young children, those children are not much better off than slaves until they grow up, even though they actually own everything their father had. They have to obey their guardians until they reach whatever age their father set. And that's the way it was with us before Christ came. We were like children; we were slaves to the basic spiritual principles of this world. But when the right time came, God sent his Son, born of a woman, subject to the law. God sent him to buy freedom for us who were slaves to the law so that he could adopt us as his very own children. And because we are his children, God has sent the Spirit of his Son into our hearts, prompting us to call out, "Abba, Father." Now you are no longer a slave but God's own child. And since you are his child, God has made you his heir."

Sarah represents the Jerusalem from above (Galatians 4:26), described in Revelation 21, the one that Hebrews 11:10 NIV describes as *"the city with foundations, whose architect and builder is God."*

Those who live by faith are children of Abraham (Galatians 3:7). Therefore, those who placed their faith in Jesus Christ are descendants of Abraham and consequently *"heirs according to the promise"* (Galatians 3:29) [That all who have faith in Jesus are blessed by being justified before God].

The Law was given alongside the promise until the "child promised had come" to whom the promise was made:

> *Galatians 3:16 NIV "the promises were spoken to Abraham and to his seed. Scripture does not say" and to the seeds: meaning many people, but "and to your seed" meaning one person, who is Christ."*

The Law was given to show people their sins. It was given to direct people towards Christ because only in Him can we be freed from sin's bondage.

> *Galatians 3:19 NLT "Why, then, was the law given? It was given alongside the promise to show people their sins. But the law was designed to last only until the coming of the child who was promised [...]."*

Since Christ died for our sins and was resurrected for our justification (Romans 4:25), we are no longer under the Law (no longer 'working' for our salvation), and the only way to salvation is through Him by faith (because He is the only one who observed the law perfectly and by placing our faith in Him, His perfect obedience is imputed into us):

> *Acts 4:12 NLT "There is salvation in no one else! God has given no other name under heaven by which we must be saved."*

God, in His everlasting love and mercy, sent His only Son to die in our place so that whoever believes in Him shall not perish but have eternal life (John 3:16).

> *PHILIPPIANS 2:6-11 NLT: "Though he was God, he did not think of equality with God as something to cling*

to. Instead, he gave up his divine privileges; he took the humble position of a slave and was born as a human being.

When he appeared in human form, he humbled himself in obedience to God and died a criminal's death on a cross.

Therefore, God elevated him to the place of highest honour and gave him the name above all other names, that at the name of Jesus every knee should bow, in heaven and on earth and under the earth, and every tongue declare that Jesus Christ is Lord, to the glory of God the Father."

2

THE MYSTERY OF GOD

The mystery of God, His will and plan for the universe, is Christ Himself, whom Paul of Tarsus preached about.

Christ is the one who opens the treasures of wisdom and knowledge of God (Colossians 2:2-3).

1 Corinthians 1:24 TLB "But God has opened the eyes of those called to salvation, both Jews and Gentiles, to see that Christ is the mighty power of God to save them; Christ himself is the centre of God's wise plan for their salvation."

Ephesians 3:6 NLT "And this is God's plan: Both Gentiles and Jews who believe the Good News share equally in the riches inherited by God's children. Both are part of the same body, and both enjoy the promise of blessings because they belong to Christ Jesus."

You may ask, why is this significant? well, what separated Jews and Gentiles was the Law, specifically the ceremonial laws which among other things, entailed the giving of animal sacrifices in order for their sins to be forgiven and be made right before God.

Ephesians 2:1-16 talks about this hostility and in verses 14-15 it says that Jesus ended this hostility; *"For Christ himself has brought peace to us. He united Jews and Gentiles into one people when, <u>in his own body on the cross</u>, he broke down the wall of hostility that separated us. **He did this by ending the system of law with its commandments and regulations**. He made peace between Jews and Gentiles by creating in himself one new people from the two groups."* (emphasis added by me)

By His death on the cross a new way had been made, now faith in His sacrifice was and is sufficient to save, therefore obeying the law regarding animal sacrifices (in specific) to be made right with God no longer applied because by His sacrifice we can be made right with God.

Therefore this hostility between Jews and Gentiles ended. The Jews no longer should find pride in their sacrifices and neither should they put down Gentiles for not doing them (they didn't have the law, it was only given to the Jews). Now, by both groups putting their faith in Christ, they have been united, they are one people; Christ's body.

This applies to us all, no race or rank makes us any better than others (unlike Jews who thought were better than the Gentiles for having God's law). In Christ, we can all be reconciled to God the Father, and what unites us is our faith in Jesus Christ.

As we declare Jesus as our only Saviour:

Romans 10:10 NIV "for it is with your heart that you believe and are justified, and it is with your mouth that you profess your faith and are saved."

We are declared righteous in the eyes of God, our sins are immediately and completely forgiven when you truly repent as a consequence of <u>faith in Christ</u>."

*Psalms 51:17 EXB "The sacrifice God wants is a broken spirit. God, you will not reject a heart that is **broken and sorry for sin**" (emphasis added by me).*

*Psalms 32:1 NLT "Oh, what joy for those whose **disobedience is forgiven**, whose **sin is put out of sight!**" (emphasis added by me)*

*Hebrews 4:16 NLT "So let us come boldly to the throne of our **gracious God**. There we will **receive his mercy**, and we will find grace to help us when we need it most." (emphasis added by me)*

*John 14:6 NLT "Jesus told him, "I am the way, the truth, and the life. No one can come to the Father **except through me**." (emphasis added by me)*

1 Timothy 2:5 NLT "There is one God and one Mediator who can reconcile God and humanity—the man Christ Jesus."

3

THE NECESSITY OF HAVING CHRIST

Romans 1:18-32 speaks of man's culpability. God is just by punishing people for rejecting Him because even though He has revealed Himself through nature, we have rejected Him and gone astray.

Not only have we heard the preaching of the gospel, but through creation itself by what is seen, heard and touched…those things show His power and divine nature:

Romans 1:20 NLT "For ever since the world was created, people have seen the earth and sky. Through everything God made, they can clearly see his invisible qualities—his eternal power and divine nature. So they have no excuse for not knowing God."

The Bible tells us we will not have an excuse before God for our unbelief and lack of obedience to His word.

Romans 1:21-23 NLT "Yes, they knew God, but they wouldn't worship him as God or even give him thanks. And they began to think up foolish ideas of what God was like. As a result, their minds became dark and confused. Claiming to be wise, they instead became utter fools. And instead of worshipping the glorious, ever-living God, they worshipped idols made to look like mere people and birds and animals and reptiles."

Without Jesus (John 8:12), people cannot see the light of the gospel (2 Corinthians 3:14); 2 Corinthians 4:4 NLT "Satan, who is the god of this world, has blinded the minds of those who don't believe. They are unable to see the glorious light of the Good News. They don't understand this message about the glory of Christ, who is the exact likeness of God."

> *Ephesians 4:17-19 NLT "With the Lord's authority I say this: Live no longer as the Gentiles do, for they are hopelessly confused. Their minds are full of darkness; they wander far from the **life God gives** because <u>they</u> have **closed their minds and hardened their hearts against him**. They have no sense of shame. They live for lustful pleasure and eagerly practice every kind of impurity." (emphasis added by me)*

> *Ephesians 5:14 NLT "For the light makes everything visible. This is why it is said, "Awake, O sleeper, rise up from the dead and Christ will give you light."*

> *John 9:39 AMP "Then Jesus said, "I came into this world for judgment [to separate those who believe in Me from those who reject Me—to declare judgment on those who choose to be separated from God], so that the sightless would see, and those who see would become blind."*

If you recognise that you are spiritually blind (the condition that follows the rejection of the things of God), Jesus will bring light into your life because you have recognised your state as sinful and need of a Saviour. Admitting that you are a sinner (which comes only by the Holy Spirit's conviction) is like asking for help and God coming to your rescue through the person of Jesus Christ.

If you persistently reject the good news or consider yourself spiritually superior, you are not admitting that you are blind and, therefore, cannot get help from Jesus. The light can only illuminate you if you recognise your spiritual blindness and wish to receive sight.

> *1 John 1:8-10 NLT "If we claim we have no sin, we are only fooling ourselves and not living in the truth. But if we confess our sins to him, he is faithful and just to forgive us our sins and to cleanse us from all wickedness. If we claim we have not sinned, we are calling God a liar and showing that his word has no place in our hearts."*

DISBELIEF IS NOT A CONSEQUENCE OF THE ABSENCE OF EVIDENCE, BUT THE UNWILLINGNESS TO BELIEVE.

> *Romans 1:28 NLT "Since they thought it foolish to acknowledge God, he abandoned them to their foolish thinking and let them do things that should never be done."*

When it says, "he abandoned them to their foolish thinking", it means that He allows people in their immoral and self-destructive deeds due to their persistent rejection of God.

Romans 1:21-32 describes the inevitable consequences of allowing sin to dominate your life. It begins by rejecting God; then they give into their thoughts of what a god (suitable for their lifestyle) should be like and what should do; due to a deceived mind, they fall into sin. Due to the sins committed, consequences arise, and hatred rises within their hearts for God, and they encourage others to feel the same way.

GOD DOES NOT INITIATE THE PROGRESSION TOWARDS EVIL, BUT WHEN WE CONSTANTLY CHOOSE TO IGNORE HIM AND REJECT HIM, HE ALLOWS US TO LIVE THE WAY WE CHOOSE TO PICK.

We all have the opportunity to live in the Spirit (that is guided by the Spirit of God) or in the flesh (that is let our sinful desires direct our lives).

Romans 6:23 NLT "for the wages of sin is death, but the free gift of God is eternal life through Christ Jesus our Lord."

God reveals to us the truth when we are willing to hear and receive it.

*Matthew 16:17 NLT "Jesus replied, "You are blessed, Simon son of John, because **my Father in heaven has revealed this to you**. You did not learn this from any human being." (emphasis added by me)*

*Ephesians 1:17-19 ESV "that the God of our Lord Jesus Christ, the Father of glory, may give you the **Spirit of wisdom and of revelation in the knowledge of him**, having the eyes of your hearts enlightened, that you may know what is the hope to which he has called you, what are the riches of his glorious inheritance in the saints, and what is the immeasurable greatness of his power toward us who believe, according to the working of his great might." (emphasis added by me)*

God will not force you to believe, if you persist in living according to your sinful desires, which automatically make you God's enemy (James 4:4) then He is going to respect your decision and grant you your wishes. If you choose to have no relationship with Him here on earth, why would you expect to have one in heaven?

If a random person came and knocked on your door and asked you if he or she could come in, I am certain your response would be no! Why? Because you do not KNOW the person, the exact same principle is in place here, God cannot allow you to live with Him eternally when you didn't take the chance to know Him when it was time to do so.

Matthew 7:23 NLT "But I will reply, 'I never knew you. Get away from me, you who break God's laws.'" (emphasis added by me)

Isaiah 55:6 ESV "Seek the LORD while He may be found; call upon Him while He is near."

However, Christ came to break those chains that hold us down, SIN!

1 John 3:8 NLT "but when people keep on sinning, it shows that they belong to the devil, who has been sinning since the beginning. But the Son of God came to destroy the works of the devil."

In Christ, there is salvation, restoration, healing, freedom, peace and life in abundance!

John 10:10 NLT "the thief's purpose is to steal and kill and destroy. My purpose is to give them a rich and satisfying life."

The thief here is the devil. The devil's only desire is to keep you chained and blinded so that you will not know Jesus Christ, and you may ask why? The reason is that he knows we have the opportunity to have something he will never have, SALVATION!

God choose to crush His Son (Isaiah 53:5) to grant us forgiveness of sins so that we could be free from sin and therefore live for Him through the power of His Spirit.

You may wonder why did Jesus have to die? Why not another way? The reason why it had to be Jesus is that a sinner cannot die for another sinner, and an unjust cannot save another unjust, it had to be someone perfect without sin so that the law would be satisfied in His obedience and through whom our sinfulness could be exchanged for His righteousness.

The reason why he had to die is because Romans 6:23 says that the wages of sin is death.

Romans 5:12 NKJV "Therefore, just as through one man sin entered the world, and <u>death through sin</u>, and thus death spread to all men, because all sinned." (emphasis added by me)

Therefore the only way to "pay" was through death, and in defeating death, He proved to be stronger because the wages of sin, death, didn't overcome by leaving Him dead still. His resurrection proves we also can overcome the power of death, proving sin no longer has a hold on us. However, we can choose to remain spiritually dead, that is by allowing sin to reign in us, by refusing to take the only way to salvation.

Another question you may ask yourself is why is Jesus the only way? Why aren't there more ways to heaven? But that is not the right question, the right question is why would God the creator of everything, the one sitting on the throne forever and always, who is still God no matter if we love Him or not, give us ANY chance of salvation?

We might look at criminals and think we are somehow better than they are but we are all capable of doing the same evil deeds they have done, we are all wicked whether we want to admit it or not, and we all deserve hell because we are evil by nature and we persistently choose to remain that way, so being this sinful why would God even give us any chance to enter heaven?

He does so because He loves us! Love is not always just getting what we want, love is also demonstrated through rebuke. Some people use judgment as an excuse to refuse to believe in God but if He didn't judge us for our sins, He wouldn't be a just judge.

Judgement is a way of God dealing with sin and He does this because He is holy, He hates sin!

Ephesians 2:1-5 NLT "Once you were dead because of your disobedience and your many sins. You used to live in sin, just like the rest of the world, obeying the devil- the commander of the powers in the unseen world. He is the spirit at work in the hearts of those who refuse to obey God. All of us used to live that way, following the passionate desires and inclinations of our sinful nature. By our very nature we were subject to God's anger, just like everyone else.

But God is so rich in mercy, and He loved us so much, that even though we were dead because of our sins, He gave us life when He raised Christ from the dead. (It is only by God's grace that you have been saved!)."

The sentence, "The commander of the powers in the unseen world", makes reference to how the devil is in control of the evil in the spiritual world and when someone lives far from God, that is subject to sin, they are following the devil (Ephesians 2:2).

However, it does not need to stay that way because Christ Jesus overcame his power at the cross.

Colossians 2:15 NLT "in this way, he disarmed the spiritual rulers and authorities. He shamed them publicly by his victory over them on the cross."

Before the presence of God no one is good (that is achieving moral perfection) because God is the standard of good (being morally perfect) and since no one is good, no one can earn salvation:

Ephesians 2:9 NLT "salvation is not a reward for the good things we have done, so no one of us can boast about it."

Christ paid the price, He defeated death so that we could be declared righteous before God. <u>Only by placing our faith in Him, we shall be declared righteous.</u>

There is a story in the book of Genesis (chapter 4) and it talks about two brothers, Abel and Cain. Both brought an offering to God, however only Abel's offering pleased God. The reason why is that Cain worked hard to get all the good crops and bring them to God. However, Abel only brought a lamb.

The only thing he did was take the lamb and present himself to God saying this is all I have, but Cain brought to God what his deeds had produced.

The point here is that Abel **hid behind this lamb** whereas Cain **brought His efforts**. The lamb here represents Jesus. Do not try to earn your way to heaven, it is a heavy burden that is going to end up destroying you rather than bringing you to God, just take the Lamb (John 1:29) and hide behind Him and present yourself to God, He will then see the Lamb instead of you.

> *1 Timothy 2:3-6 NLT "This is good and pleases God our Saviour, who wants everyone to be saved and to understand the truth.*
>
> *For there is one God and one Mediator who can reconcile God and humanity—the man Christ Jesus. **<u>He gave His life to purchase freedom for everyone.</u>***
>
> *This is the message God gave to the world at just the right time" (emphasis added by me).*

<u>GOD CALLS YOU TODAY TO COME TO HIM AND BE RECONCILED TO HIM THROUGH HIS SON.</u>

4

WHAT HINDERS PEOPLE FROM COMING TO CHRIST

James 4:4 NLT "You adulterers! Don't you realize that friendship with the world makes you an enemy of God? I say it again: If you want to be friend of the world, you make yourself an enemy of God."

Being friends with the world means engaging with what it has to offer, the devil is the god of this world (2 Corinthians 4:4) meaning that the world (the people, or at least the majority) serve the devil by giving into his offers which are sinful, which consequently lead to death (spiritually speaking).

Being spiritually dead means not having spiritual life within you.

1 Corinthians 15:45 NLV "The Holy Writings say, "The first man, Adam, became a living soul." But the last Adam (Christ) is a life-giving Spirit."

Christ is the only one that can give us true life; true life is a life living for God because only He satisfies our soul, therefore, giving us life, true joy and purpose.

Since Christ rose from the dead defeating death, He is the source and the means by which we can obtain **eternal life, which is true life.**

Our sinful desires prompt us to desire the sinful pleasures that this world offers, however, these pleasures of the world are sinful because they enslave us into sin's dominion. You may wonder, how can we change our desires to be Christ-centred? This comes through the renewing of our minds, which means changing the way we think. Our minds can only be renewed in Christ, once the Holy Spirit convicts us of our sin and we put our faith in Christ as Saviour. The Holy Spirit will lead us into a process called sanctification in which essentially we die to ourselves in order for more of Christ to be formed within us (Galatians 4:19).

> *Colossians 3:10 NLT "put on your new nature, and <u>be renewed</u> as you learn to <u>KNOW</u> your Creator and BECOME like Him." (emphasis added by me)*

> *Romans 12:2 NLT "Don't copy the behaviour and customs of this world, but <u>let God transform you</u> into a new person <u>by changing the way you think.</u> Then you will learn to know God's will for you, which is good and pleasing and perfect." (emphasis added by me)*

The keywords in these verses are to know, become and transform. If we made these three words the rules of our lives, our lives would be very different.

To know someone requires experiences with the person, and intimacy (getting to know them at their deepest) and it requires effort and commitment, you may not always feel like talking to them but because you love them, you choose them.

It is like a parent-child relationship, the parents don't just leave their child whenever they behave badly because they are committed to their role as parents and they love their child. The same principle applies to God, when life is hard we don't just give up, we chose to commit to Him the day we put our faith in Christ and that day, we made a vow before His presence that we choose to willingly give all we are to Him.

To become means to change, to grow to be. This can only be done by abiding in Jesus (John 15:5) and through the power of the Holy Spirit.

For those who do not know Jesus, <u>you can become a child of God through what **He** has already done</u>. All you have to do <u>is put your faith in what He has already done, which is sufficient to save.</u>

To transform is to change, which can only be done by the power of the Holy Spirit. Similar to becoming, you don't become something unless you are transformed.

Only when someone has been transformed by God can he or she think the way God desires, and His will for your life even though it will be full of trials to test your faith, will satisfy you.

As you keep living embracing the sinful pleasures of this world you are dominated by sin.

*Romans 6:16 NLT "Don't you realize that you become the slave of whatever you choose to obey? You can be a slave to sin, which leads to death, **or you can choose to obey God, which leads to righteous living."** (Emphasis added by me)*

Ephesians 2:2 NLT "You used to live in sin, just like the rest of the world, obeying the devil—the commander of the powers in the unseen world. He is the spirit at work in the hearts of those who refuse to obey God."

It makes sense that only someone stronger could defeat that whom has him or her held in bondage. How could we possibly be stronger than sin? If we were, there would be no need for Jesus to come and die for the sins of the world…

Mark 3:27 NLT "Let me illustrate this further. Who is powerful enough to enter the house of a strong man and plunder his goods? Only someone even stronger—someone who could tie him up and then plunder his house."

1 John 3:4-8 NLT "Everyone who sins is breaking God's law, for all sin is contrary to the law of God. <u>And you know that Jesus came to take away our sins, and there is no sin in him</u>. Anyone who continues to live in him will not sin. But *anyone who keeps on sinning does not know him or understand who he is.*

Dear children, don't let anyone deceive you about this: When people do what is right, it shows that they are righteous, even as Christ is righteous. <u>But when people keep on sinning, it shows that they belong to the devil, who has been sinning since the beginning. But the Son of God came to destroy the works of the devil.</u> (Emphasis added by me)

Romans 7:23-24 NLT "But there is another power within me that is at war with my mind. This power makes me a slave to the sin that is still within me. Oh, what a miserable person I am! Who will free me from this life that is dominated by sin and death?."

*Romans 6:12-13 NLT "Do not let sin control the way you live; do not give in to sinful desires. Do not let any part of your body become an instrument of evil to serve sin. **Instead, give yourselves completely to God**, for you were dead, but now you have new life. So use your whole body as an instrument to do what is right for the glory of God." (Emphasis added by me)*

Romans 6:13 and 16 give us the solution to this bondage; GIVE OURSELVES TO GOD because only He can save you, transform you, heal you, satisfy you and most importantly give you eternal life!

*Romans 6:19 MSG "I'm using this freedom language because it's easy to picture. You can readily recall, can't you, how at one time **the more you did just what you felt like doing—not caring about others, not caring about God—the worse your life became and the less freedom you had**? And how much different is it now as you live in God's freedom, your lives healed and expansive in holiness?" (emphasis added by me)*

The Bible repeatedly shows us the way out of this bondage to sin.

*Romans 7:25 NLT "Thank God! The answer is in **Jesus Christ** our Lord. So you see how it is: In my mind, I really want to obey God's law, but **because of my sinful nature I am a slave to sin.**" (emphasis added by me)*

God commands us to abstain from the pleasures this world offers, not because He wants all the attention and wants to deprive us of happiness or pleasures. He does so because He knows that what our soul needs is Him because only He can satisfy what every human is after.

Our desires are against His desires for us, and our desires only lead us to sin (Romans 8:7) which consequently leads us to spiritual death. However, life with Him leads to peace, joy, love, satisfaction, fulfilment and eternal life. Worshipping God and living for Him doesn't make Him more or less God, He is still on the throne and is worthy of praise regardless of whether we give it or not, but in doing so, we are benefiting ourselves because the purpose of our existence is to live for Him.

James 4:4 NLT "You adulterers! Don't you realise that friendship with the world makes you an enemy of God? I say it again: If you want to be a friend of the world, you make yourself an enemy of God."

As we all have sinned and made this world our home, we all fall into this category of God's enemies.

Yet God gives us the way out to freedom once again. James 4:7 *"So humble yourselves before God. Resist the devil, and he will flee from you."*

Notice how this verse starts with humbling ourselves before God. We must recognize our sin (conviction comes from the Holy Spirit), our need for a Saviour and our inability to save ourselves and this requires us to die to our ego and humble ourselves.

1 John 1:8-10 AMP "If we say we have no sin [refusing to admit that we are sinners], we delude ourselves and the truth is not in us. [His word does not live in our hearts.] If we [freely] admit that we have sinned and confess our sins, He is faithful and just [true to His own nature and promises], and will forgive our sins and cleanse us continually from all unrighteousness [our wrongdoing, everything not in conformity with His will and purpose]. If we say that we have not sinned [refusing to admit acts of sin], we make Him [out to be] a liar [by contradicting Him] and His word is not in us."

Those who are friends with the world are under the devil's dominion:

1 John 3:8 NLT " But when people keep on sinning, it shows that they belong to the devil, who has been sinning since the beginning [...]"

Witnessing our state God didn't abandon us:

1 John 3:8 NLT "But the Son of God came to destroy the works of the devil."

Ephesians 2:4-5 NLT "But God is so rich in mercy, and he loved us so much, that even though we were dead because of our sins, he gave us life when he raised Christ from the dead. (It is only by God's grace that you have been saved!)."

Christianity may appear to be a set of rules to follow to achieve heaven. However, that is the biggest lie. What makes Christianity different from all the other religions is the essence of a relationship, a Father-son/daughter relationship. Looking back on where God took me out, I remember how lonely and empty I felt and how all I wanted was someone to love me as I was with all my defects and my mistakes (He takes us as we are, yet God call us out of sin and into holiness- John 8:10-11), someone who would never leave me! And I tried in many ways to find that fulfilment in people, drinking, dating, etc., but no one could do what only God can.

Another difference between Christianity and the other religions is that salvation is not earned nor achieved by any of our efforts;

Luke 1:77 NLT "You [John the Baptist] will tell his people how to <u>find</u> salvation through forgiveness of their sins." (emphasis added by me).

It is found, it is received but never earned nor worked for by our own efforts.

Romans 10:8 NLT "In fact it says, 'The message is very close at hand; it is on your lips and in your heart[...].'" (referring to how salvation is as close to us as our own lips and heart are. <u>The only means by which we are saved is by placing our faith in Christ Jesus alone, by grace alone</u>). (emphasis added by me)

*Ephesians 2:8-9 NLT "**God saved you** by **his grace** when you **believed**. And **you can't take credit for this**; it is a **gift from God**. Salvation is **not a reward** for the good things we have done, so none of us can boast about it." (emphasis added by me).*

*1 Corinthians 1:31 "Let the one who boasts, **boast in the Lord.**" (emphasis added by me).*

When we give our lives to Christ, life changes completely. His presence attracts you; you cannot taste who He is and be left the same. Once you taste a glimpse of His glory, your soul will cry out for more because He is the lover of your soul.

Psalm 34:8 "Taste and see that the LORD is good [...]"

Life with Christ does not mean there will be an end to all your problems or no illness or no distress, it just means that there will always be someone who will fight for you and take you through the pain. Pain is necessary as hard as it is to admit (Psalm 119:71).

He won't exempt you from pain because life is bound to pain. However, He will be your helper through your every distress.

As you read the pages of this book, the devil is scheming against you and how to deceive you and steal what God is planting in your heart through these words (Matthew 13:19). God is calling you to be reconciled to Him now, don't let the devil rob you from what can be yours if you place your faith in Jesus Christ; SALVATION.

One of the devil's purposes is to blind you to the truth.

2 Corinthians 4:4 NLT "Satan, who is the god of this world, has blinded the minds of those who don't believe. They are unable to see the glorious light of the Good News. They don't understand this message about the glory of Christ, who is the exact likeness of God." God wants to remove this veil so that you can live for Him, in freedom and confidence in the hope of eternal life.

*2 Corinthians 3:14-16 NLT "But the people's minds were hardened, and to this day whenever the old covenant is being read, the same veil covers their minds so they cannot understand the truth. And **this veil can be removed only by believing in Christ**. Yes, even today when they read Moses' writings, their hearts are covered with that veil, and they do not understand. **But whenever someone turns to the Lord, the veil is taken away.**" (emphasis added by me)*

You may ask, why should I live a life that pleases God? Isn't it my life? Shouldn't I get to decide what to do with it? And the answer is yes, you can do what you want when you want the way you want to (1 Corinthians 10:23); however, you cannot live as an enemy of God and yet expect to inherit what is due to His children, i.e., heaven. A life lived for God is not a life wasted, it's a life lived to the fullest. A life full of joy, freedom, peace, salvation, love… things which living a life devoted to satisfy one's whims does not provide.

> *Revelation 21:27 NLT "Nothing evil will be allowed to enter, nor anyone who practices shameful idolatry and dishonesty—but only those whose names are written in the Lamb's Book of Life."*

God wants us to live a life that pleases Him because that's the kind of life that will bring Him glory and the type of life that will fill that void we are so busy trying to fill. If you don't believe me, look at all those famous people who end up taking their own lives or who end up dead because of drugs or alcohol or money. If life is all about now and having as much as I can to please myself, shouldn't they be the happiest? Should they not want to give that up?

However, we read that Paul estimated everything else as garbage compared to knowing Christ. Also, in the book of Revelation, we read how martyrs were willing to lose their lives for Jesus's sake. If life here is all that matters why were they willing to lose it, what did they love more than their own lives?

> *Revelation 12:11 NLT "[…] and they did not love their lives so much that they were afraid to die."*

Paul lived a life of horror, persecution, criticism, loneliness, homelessness, etc. However, he was willing to go through all of that, why? Why give up so much having everything other people esteemed as valuable at that time? Paul was a pharisee, which at that time was the top rank, spiritually speaking. He was a Jew, of the tribe of Benjamin, circumcised (which was very important in those times)… everything that made a Jew someone of honour he had, and he gave it all up because of just one encounter with the Risen Christ (Acts 9:3-6). That's all it took! Yet he was never left the same.

The pleasures of this world; fame, wealth, popularity, best job, best car, etc.… all seem to have captivated our society, but in what we think there is freedom, the word of God says it leads to slavery.

Romans 7:9-11 NLT "At one time I lived without understanding the law. But when I learned the command not to covet, for instance, the power of sin came to life, and I died. So I discovered that the law's commands, which were supposed to bring life, brought spiritual death instead. Sin took advantage of those commands and deceived me; it used the commands to kill me."

We covet other people's lives or assets even on social media nowadays. We covet their lives, car, financial status, etc. By desiring all these things, which we believe will lead to happiness and true life, we actually end up being slaves to our desires, always wanting more.

When it says that the power of sin came to life, it means that through the law, which was supposed to highlight his sinful nature (because of our inability to obey the law perfectly) and to point him to Christ (because He did obey the law perfectly), sin took advantage and awoke desires in him that were against the law.

*Romans 7:13 NLT "But how can that be? Did the law, which is good, cause my death? Of course not! Sin used what was good to bring about my condemnation to death. So **we can see how terrible sin really is**. It uses God's good commands for its own evil purposes." (emphasis added by me)*

Simply put, it is like when people say that the more you prohibit something from someone, the more they want it. Basically when the law said do not covet it awoke that desire in him and caused him to, therefore, be spiritually dead.

Sin dwelling inside of us will begin to dominate. In the Scriptures sin is sometimes personified, it seems like essentially the more we give in to sin's influence on our lives, i.e., give in to our desires, the more enslaved we become.

Genesis 4:7 NLT "You will be accepted if you do what is right. But if you refuse to do what is right, then watch out! ***Sin is crouching at the door, eager to control you. But you must subdue it and be its master." ***(emphasis added by me)*

Romans 7:17-20 NLT "So I am not the one doing wrong; it is sin living in me that does it. And I know that nothing good lives in me, that is, in my sinful nature. I want to do what is right, but I can't. I want to do what is good, but I don't. I don't want to do what is wrong, but I do it anyway. But if I do what I don't want to do, I am not really the one doing wrong; it is sin living in me that does it."

Freedom from and authority to subdue sin are given in Jesus Christ.

Romans 8:3 NLT "The law of Moses was unable to save us because of the weakness of our sinful nature. So ***God did*** *what the law could not do.* ***He sent his own Son in a body like the bodies we sinners have. And in that body God declared an end to sin's control over us by giving his Son as a sacrifice for our sins****." (emphasis added by me)*

Notice the fact that it says God did, God sent. The Bible tells us that there is nothing <u>we can do</u> to be free from sin's dominion and to obtain eternal life. It is all given.

Your lifestyle shows whether you live dominated by sin; your desires, the places you frequent, the things you watch… all of those things reveal whom you serve.

Romans 8:5-7 NLT "Those who <u>*are dominated by the sinful nature*</u> *think about sinful things, but those who are controlled by the Holy Spirit think about things that please the Spirit. So letting your sinful nature control your mind leads to death. But letting the Spirit control your mind leads to life and peace. For the sinful nature is always hostile to God. It never did obey God's laws, and it never will." (emphasis added by me)*

Romans 8:12-13 NLT "Therefore, dear brothers and sisters, you have no obligation to do what your sinful nature urges you to do. For if you live by its dictates, you will die. But if through the power of the Spirit you put to death the deeds of your sinful nature, you will live."

For those who have placed their faith in Jesus, I will discuss a few verses that should lead us to meditate on our Christian lives. However, they can also speak to those who don't know Him yet.

Matthew 7:21-23 NLT "Not everyone who calls out to me, 'Lord! Lord!' will enter the Kingdom of Heaven. Only those who actually <u>do the will of my Father</u> in heaven will enter. On judgment day many will say to me, 'Lord! Lord! We <u>prophesied</u> in your name, cast out demons, and <u>performed</u> many miracles in your name.' But I will reply, '<u>I never knew you</u>. Get away from me, you who break God's laws." (emphasis added by me)

I would like to slowly dissect this part of scripture and analyse the important elements. First, notice how it emphasises that only those who OBEY will enter the kingdom of heaven. It is important to realise that obedience to God only comes as a result of being saved. Only a transformed heart, by the grace of God, can follow and desire to please God. Once your life belongs to Christ, a true believer will <u>respond</u> to His grace by obeying, that's why obedience is always directly linked to love because biblical love is shown by actions. Evidence and not just words.

If you notice, the people in these verses said we performed, cast out, prophesied… ACTION WORDS. As I discussed, actions can show your love for God, but sometimes they are deceiving. For example, the Pharisees professed to know and love God, yet their hatred for "sinners" (thinking as if they were saints) directly contradicts God's command to love others and to show mercy.

My point is that <u>they based their salvation on what they did</u>. Your works won't save you, only faith in Christ will.

Lastly, Jesus responded, " I DON'T KNOW YOU." I don't know about you but these words cause my soul to tremble. Jesus essentially said we don't have a relationship. Of course Jesus knows who they are. Through Him, all things were made according to Colossians 1:16. He meant that there is no intimacy, no friendship, no personal experience, or no encounter with them.

Luke 7:47 NLT "I tell you, her sins—and they are many—have been forgiven, so she has shown me much love. But a person who is forgiven little shows only little love."

Only those who know how much has been forgiven will respond with a devoted life of surrender.

5

IF I BECOME A CHRISTIAN DOES IT MEAN I WON'T SIN ANYMORE?

*1 John 1:5-9 NLT "This is the message we heard from Jesus and now declare to you: God is light, and there is no darkness in him at all. So **we are lying if we say we have fellowship with God but go on living in spiritual darkness**; we are not practising the truth. But if we are living in the light, as God is in the light, then we have fellowship with each other, and the blood of Jesus, his Son, cleanses us from all sin.*

If we claim we have no sin, we are only fooling ourselves and not living in the truth. But if we confess our sins to him, he is faithful and just to forgive us our sins and to cleanse us from all wickedness." (emphasis added by me)

If we claim to know and follow Christ, then our desires have changed. We are new creatures.

2 Corinthians 5:17 NLT "This means that anyone who belongs to Christ has become a new person. The old life is gone; a new life has begun!"

John 3:3 NLT "Jesus replied, "I tell you the truth, unless you are born again, you cannot see the Kingdom of God."

Once we place our faith in Christ, we are made new. The Holy Spirit lives in us and begins the work of sanctification within us, which is making us more like Jesus (1 Peter 1:15-16). We now live differently, we desire different things, and we desire God and to follow His ways.

Ezekiel 36:26-27 NLT "And I will give you a new heart, and I will put a new spirit in you. I will take out your stony, stubborn heart and give you a tender, responsive heart. And I will put my Spirit in you so that you will follow my decrees and be careful to obey my regulations."

2 Corinthians 5:9 NLT "So whether we are here in this body or away from this body, our goal is to please him."

John 15:16 ESV "You did not choose me, but I chose you and appointed you that you should go and bear fruit and that your fruit should abide, so that whatever you ask the Father in my name, he may give it to you."

Colossians 1:10 ESV "So as to walk in a manner worthy of the Lord, fully pleasing to him: bearing fruit in every good work and increasing in the knowledge of God."

When someone puts their faith in Jesus for salvation, one doesn't change straight away and never sins again. However, there is a change of heart, the Holy Spirit is within you, changing your heart as you learn more of God by reading the Bible and your desires naturally will change and will lead you to a life of obedience to God, out of love.

It is a response, not a requirement for salvation.

It's a response to who He is. Having encountered Him you just want more of Him which eventually leads to a changed life.

1 John 3:5-9 NLT "And you know that <u>Jesus came to take away our sins</u>, and there is no sin in him. Anyone who continues to live in him will not sin. But anyone who keeps on sinning does not know him or understand who he is.

Dear children, don't let anyone deceive you about this: When people do what is right, it shows that they are righteous, even as Christ is righteous But when people keep on sinning, it shows that they belong to the devil, who has been sinning since the beginning. But the Son of God came to destroy the works of the devil. Those who have been born into God's family do not make a practice of sinning, because God's life is in them. So they can't keep on sinning, because they are children of God" (emphasis added by me).

Let's dissect this passage in order to receive all the goodness God has in these verses. First, when it says "will not sin", it does NOT mean that Christians don't sin at all and that they are perfect. Far from that! What it is saying is that Christians don't make sinning a practice, a lifestyle. They're not indifferent to God's law.

They do fall. The difference between someone who is saved and someone who is not is that when they sin, their heart grieves and becomes contrite because they have realised they have sinned against the One they love, a Holy God. This is seen in Psalms 51, where David, who was a man after God's own heart (Acts 13:22), repented from a terrible sin he had committed against God. If you think Christians claim to be perfect and better than everyone let me show you something that will disprove your theory.

David didn't just mess up, he slipped and hit hard! He had committed adultery and planned for the woman's husband to get killed at war. He basically arranged his death after taking his wife!! And if you read the account in 2 Samuel 11, you will see that the woman's husband was actually very faithful to king David, which just made his sin even worse!!

Now reading the Psalm, you will be amazed by David's repentant heart and unwillingness to give up on following God. He had suffered a dear consequence because of his sin, the son he had with the woman died. However, it is evident that David suffered more from hurting God's heart than from the loss of his son.

In his story, we can see the effect sinning has on those who do belong to God. They don't just become indifferent and be like 'oh well I'm just weak'. No, they become contrite, and their hearts are filled with sorrow because they have offended their first love! And as crazy as it sounds that's what should happen, so if we claim to know Jesus but we are indifferent when we sin towards Him then we should really question if we even encountered Him in the first place!

Continuing with the passage in 1 John 3, it says *"when people do what is right, they show they are righteous."* This means that they seek to live according to God's ways. They desire to please Him with their life because pleasing Him satisfies their heart.

Do you desire to obey God? Is your desire to follow after His desires for you even if it means giving up your own? What do you desire the most in this life?

6

SPIRITUAL BLINDNESS

If we live life to satisfy our selfish and sinful desires, with no regard for God and His word, we will receive what we so wished for, separation from God. View it in this way, the outcome of a life separated from God is an eternity separated from God. We cannot expect to receive benefits from someone we were not willing to commit to. In the same way, <u>we cannot live as enemies of God and expect to receive the inheritance that belongs to His children.</u>

Matthew 10:28 NLT "Don't be afraid of those who want to kill your body; they cannot touch your soul. Fear only God, who can destroy both soul and body in hell."

When Jesus was on this earth, He preached about hell more than He did about heaven. Is a topic that is not welcomed but we must hear it because this is a matter of life and death, which involves your eternal destiny and soul, which are of great value to God. Nothing is more valuable than your soul.

Matthew 16:26 NLT "And what do you benefit if you gain the whole world but lose your own soul? Is anything worth more than your soul?"

According to that verse, gaining the whole word does not compare to losing your soul. That shows the immense value of your soul, the life of Christ.

1 Peter 1:18-19 NLT "For you know that God paid a ransom to save you from the empty life you inherited from your ancestors. And it was not paid with mere gold or silver, which lose their value. It was the precious blood of Christ, the sinless, spotless Lamb of God."

The reason why God keeps calling us to repentance is not to deprive us of good things as many people think, for God is the giver of good things (James 1:17). But because He cares for you, He warns you persistently!

*2 Peter 3:9 NLT "The Lord isn't really being slow about his promise, as some people think. No, he is being **patient** for your sake. He does not want anyone to be destroyed, but **wants everyone to repent**." (emphasis added by me)*

1 Timothy 2:4 NLT "Who wants everyone to be saved and to understand the truth."

You may wonder if God is love, then why is He going to judge the world? The answer is in Genesis 6.

In Genesis 6 we are told about the story of a man called Noah, whom God had called to build an ark to be saved from the coming judgment.

Genesis 6:5-8 NLT "The Lord observed the extent of human wickedness on the earth, and he saw that everything they thought or imagined was consistently and totally evil. So the Lord was sorry he had ever made them and put them on the earth. It broke his heart. And the Lord said, "I will wipe this human race I have created from the face of the earth. Yes, and I will destroy every living thing—all the people, the large animals, the small animals that scurry along the ground, and even the birds of the sky. I am sorry I ever made them." But Noah found favour with the Lord."

Before I discuss the reasoning behind the future judgment I need to clarify what it means when it said God was sorry for creating us. The use of speech in this verse is called anthropopathism, which is the appliance of human emotions or thought processing to the infinite God for us to gain a better understanding. God did not regret creating humanity otherwise we wouldn't be here right now. The use of anthropopathism shows us in these verses that God felt sorrow over the direction humans were taking, which was towards evil. It also highlights the sorrow He felt as He saw us choosing sin over Him. This raises a very important question within me… How could something that causes sorrow to God's heart bring joy or satisfaction to mine? (if I claim to know Christ) How can sin, being so displeasing to God, bring pleasure to my life …?

This is what causes God's wrath to be built upon us.

> *Colossians 3:5-6 NLT "So put to death the **sinful, earthly things lurking within you**. Have nothing to do with sexual immorality, impurity, lust, and evil desires. Don't be greedy, for a greedy person is an idolater, worshipping the things of this world. Because of these sins, the anger of God is coming." (emphasis added by me)*

The sinful, earthly things arise within us from the dominion of our sinful nature upon our lives which has been discussed previously. Choosing to live a life with no regard towards God, even though He is consistently warning us to turn from sin because He knows that it desires to dominate and destroy us, is what causes the wrath of God to one day be unleashed upon humanity; **Our rebellion**.

> *2 Thessalonians 1:7-9 NLT "And God will provide rest for you who are being persecuted and also for us when the Lord Jesus appears from heaven. He will come with his mighty angels, in flaming fire, bringing judgment on **those who don't know God and on those who refuse to obey the Good News of our Lord Jesus**. They will be punished with eternal destruction, forever separated from the Lord and from his glorious power." (emphasis added by me)*

I know that reading that sounds pretty harsh but the words here are very simple. Those who do not know God and those who refuse to obey the good news of Jesus Christ (believe in it) will be punished because they remain in the state of condemnation and refuse to take the way out of this state; Jesus Christ.

Some people think that we need to commit these terrible sins like murder, rape, etc… for us to not go to heaven, that only those people are evil enough not to deserve it. However, we are ALL capable of horrific acts, not because you don't murder means you are better or more worthy of heaven than murderers because you and I are just as capable of such acts as those who commit them.

Those people who might think that they are the "furthest" from heaven may be the closest. What I mean by that is the following;

*Matthew 21:31 NLT "Which of the two obeyed his father?" They replied, "The first." Then Jesus explained his meaning: "**I tell you the truth, corrupt tax collectors and prostitutes will get into the Kingdom of God before you do.**" (emphasis added by me)*

The Pharisees thought they were closer to God because they studied the law, knew it completely and prayed for long hours. However, Jesus said that those who were the most rejected were closer to heaven than those who claimed it for themselves.

The reason why is very simple!

*Matthew 21:32 NLT "For John the Baptist came and showed you the right way to live, but you **didn't believe** him, while tax collectors and prostitutes did. And even when you saw this happening, **you refused to believe him and repent of your sins**." (emphasis added by me)*

It is important to notice that John was pointing people to Jesus, that is why here it says they didn't believe him, because they didn't believe the message he preached and that was JESUS!

His message can be read in Matthew 3:1-12 (NLT), however, I want to point out the main body of this message.

*Matthew 3:1-12 (NLT) "**Repent of your sins and turn to God**, for the Kingdom of Heaven is near" (verse 2) / "Prove by the way you live that you have **repented of your sins and turned to God**" (verse 8) / "I baptize with water those who **repent of their sins and turn to God**. But someone is coming soon who is greater than I am—so much greater that I'm not worthy even to be his slave and carry his sandals." (verse 11) (emphasis added by me)*

Acts 20 summarises the gospel very clearly:

*Acts 20:21 NLT "I have had one message for Jews and Greeks alike—the **necessity of repenting from sin** and **turning to God**, and of **having faith in our Lord Jesus**." (emphasis added by me)*

Why did Jesus say that the most rejected would enter heaven before they would, and also who are "they" (in Matthew 21:31)? Well if you read verse 23 of Matthew 21, Jesus was talking to the elders and priests, so it seems he referred this story to them. Jesus had previously told them this story of two sons, one who said he would help his father and he didn't and the other one said no at first but he went after, and so Jesus asked which one obeyed? They answered the second one.

This all reveals that the elders and priests believed to be the sons that obeyed God, however, they didn't. What made a vital difference between them and those looked down upon by them was **belief** (in Jesus and His words) according to Matthew 21:32.

The famous verse of John 3:16 confirms it, only those who BELIEVE will not perish but have everlasting life.

Now, it is clear that unbelief is a reason behind God's wrath. However, 2 Thessalonians 1:7-9 also mentions those who refused to obey the good news. <u>Obedience doesn't save you</u>, but it does reflect whether you know God or not. Love and obedience are tightly connected in the Scriptures. Jesus loved the Father so much that He obeyed even to the point of dying on the cross, so here we see <u>Jesus' love for the Father manifested in His obedience</u>. His faith led to fruitfulness.

If we go back to Genesis 4:1:

*"Adam **knew** Eve his wife, and she **conceived and bore** Cain." (emphasis added by me)*

There is a big difference between knowing about God and knowing God. Here the level of intimacy that Adam had with Eve led to fruitfulness. The same principle applies to our relationship with God. We should be so close to God, e.g. through prayer, studying the Word, fasting, and in community, etc that we bear fruit.

Their intimacy was evident by her fruit, the same principle applies to our relationship with God.

Repentance (*metanoia*- change of mind) and our relationship with God are <u>evident</u> (not maintained) through our fruits. That is why John said in Matthew 3:8:

Matthew 3:8 NLT "prove by the way you live you have REPENTED FROM YOUR SINS and TURNED TO GOD." (emphasis added by me)

Repentance is a change of direction away from sin to God. Turning to God is to place one's faith in Christ Jesus.

*John 14:6 NLT "Jesus told him, "I am the way, the truth, and the life. **No one can come to the Father except through me**." (emphasis added by me)*

Faith that produces no works is dead (James 2), which means that genuine faith is <u>accompanied</u> by regeneration, i.e., our minds have been renewed, we see Christ as precious and sin as something to abhor, our hearts have been changed resulting in new desires and therefore, changed behaviour.

Bringing it back to why the ones looked down upon, according to Jesus, were closest to heaven it's because of what is described in John chapter nine.

*John 9:35-41 NLT " When Jesus heard what had happened, he found the man and asked, "Do you **believe** in the Son of Man?" The man answered, "Who is he, sir? I want to believe in him." "You have **seen** him," Jesus said, "and he is speaking to you!"*

*"Yes, Lord, I believe!" the man said. And he worshipped Jesus. Then Jesus told him, "I entered this world to render judgment—to **give sight to the blind and to show those who think they see that they are blind**."*

Some Pharisees who were standing nearby heard him and asked, "Are you saying we're blind?"

*"If you were blind, you wouldn't be guilty," Jesus replied. **"But you remain guilty because you claim you can see**." (emphasis added by me)*

This passage is titled Spiritual Blindness. According to 2 Corinthians 4:4 unbelievers are blinded, and only Jesus can take that veil for them to see (2 Corinthians 3:14,16).

They were unable to see the references to Jesus as they read the Scriptures, which back then they only had the old testament.

Previously to the passage of John 9, Jesus had healed a blind man but the Pharisees and the Jewish leaders refused to believe that Jesus healed him, they claimed that it was all made up and that the man was never even blind in the first place. This principle is crucial to understand the passage that I have provided of John 9. Their refusal to believe that Jesus healed the man was the very thing that kept them blind. Blind to see that Jesus had come to this world to bring healing, not just physical but spiritual. They claimed to be spiritually "healthy" and with no need to receive sight.

However, Jesus said He brings healing to those who recognise that they are blind. Once this is recognised, we know that we cannot obtain sight by ourselves, but that someone else, greater than who is keeping us from seeing, needs to do it for us.

This is what made those looked down upon by the Pharisees closer to heaven, the fact that they could see their need for someone to give them sight, which is spiritual healing. They believed Jesus was the One who could give them sight.

Spiritual healing is the ability to see Jesus, and according to the passages provided only Jesus himself can do such a thing.

Something else that I wanted to emphasise from the passage in John 9 is the fact that the man believed and his reaction was worship. It is important to notice that after believing there was a reaction, and that that reaction was worship, which is more than singing to God, but it is a lifestyle of surrender and obedience to the One we claim to be the greatest and the object of our worship.

7

GOD'S WARNINGS

As you read this book you may wonder, why talk so much about judgement? And the reason is that even Jesus himself spoke more about hell than about heaven.

Let's consider the word "saved" for a second. Ask yourself this question, what does Jesus save people from? And that is what will be discussed in this chapter.

First, I will write it in simple words and it will be discussed in more detail along the way. First, Jesus frees us from the bondage and penalty of sin.

*Romans 6:16-18 NLT "Don't you realize that you become the slave of whatever you choose to obey? You can be a **slave to sin, which leads to death, or you can choose to obey God, which leads to righteous living.** Thank God! Once you were slaves of sin, but now you wholeheartedly obey this teaching we have given you. Now you are free from your **slavery to sin**, and you have become slaves to righteous living." (emphasis added by me)*

According to these verses we are either slaves to sin or slaves of Christ (Romans 6:22). Being a slave of Christ means to serve him, which means to live a life that brings Him glory and that is according to His will because His ways are greater than ours and His plans are far greater than our own (Isaiah 55:8-9).

Secondly, Jesus delivers us from God's wrath.

*1 Thessalonians 1:10 ESV "and to wait for his Son from heaven, whom he raised from the dead, **Jesus who delivers us from the wrath to come**." (emphasis added by me)*

*Romans 5:9 ESV "Since, therefore, we have now been justified by his blood, much more shall we be **saved by him from the wrath of God**." (emphasis added by me)*

We have previously talked about belief, believing that only Jesus can provide freedom from sin and forgiveness for our sins.

If we choose to live a life where we give way to our sinful desires, with no regard for God and His justice then, as the Bible states, our reward will be eternal death (Romans 6:23). But if instead, we place our faith in what Jesus has done, which is enough to save us and to enable us to have a relationship with the Father, then our reward shall be eternal life (Romans 6:23).

I am not trying to scare you, I only want to tell you the truth. People think they can live whatever way they want and still expect God to receive them in His kingdom after a life of full neglect towards Him. Therefore, it must be made known to you the consequences of your choice, so that people don't respond with "well, I didn't know."

A life with no regard for God equates to an eternity without God. A life of surrender to God equates to an eternity with God. Is fair to say that you would not allow a stranger to come into your house, the same principle applies to God's kingdom.

Let's begin with the reasoning as to why God is so persistent with repentance.

Perhaps your only view of God is that He is love. You are not wrong! However, He also is a hundred percent Holy and Just. He considers sin an abomination that must be punished. When we create a false image of who God is we are being idolaters since we are not following the true God, but the god that satisfies our desires.

However, love is misunderstood in today's world. Love is not saying yes to everything we want, and is not agreeing with everything we feel. Biblical love is described in 1 Corinthians 13:4-8. In these verses, it says that love rejoices in TRUTH. Therefore, **biblical love is all about truth**, not feelings.

Discipline is also a sign of love. The opposite of love it's not hate, but indifference. If we love someone, we care about them enough to call them out when they are going in the wrong direction. Similarly, God cares about our eternal destination and therefore, He must call out our sin.

> *Genesis 19:14 NLT "So Lot rushed out to tell his daughters' fiancés, "Quick, get out of the city! The Lord is about to destroy it." But the young men thought he was only joking."*

In these verses, a man called Lot is warning his daughters' fiancés to leave the country in which they were living because God was going to destroy it due to their sins (Genesis 18:20-21). However, they didn't listen and chose to remain there. **They faced God's judgment because they choose to ignore God's warnings.**

This happens daily, God speaks to individuals saying "come to Me, today is the day of salvation."

> *2 Corinthians 6:2 NLT "For God says, "At just the right time, I heard you. On the day of salvation, I helped you." Indeed, **the "right time" is now. Today is the day of salvation." (emphasis added by me)***

However, many choose to ignore it, either thinking He will never punish them and that they can get away with their sin (Psalm 50:21) or that there is still time for His judgments to come.

God desires for everyone to be saved (2 Peter 3:9, 1 Timothy 2:4, Ezekiel 18:23). But we keep ignoring His warnings, people can no longer keep thinking that it's okay to just keep on sinning with no consequences and then expect heaven. It just doesn't work that way, so this is why I need to tell you the truth.

Now, I know the bad news sounds terrible but there can be a good ending to your story. Usually, stories talk about villains and heroes. Well, in the story of humanity, we are the villains and Jesus is the hero.

*1 John 2:2 TLB "**He is the one who took God's wrath against our sins upon himself** and brought us into fellowship with God, and **he is the forgiveness for our sins**, and not only ours but all the world's." (emphasis added by me)*

Romans 5:8 TLB "But God showed his great love for us by sending Christ to die for us while we were still sinners."

*Romans 7:24-25 NLT "Oh, what a miserable person I am! Who will free me from this life that is dominated by sin and death? Thank God! **The answer is in Jesus Christ our Lord** [...]" (emphasis added by me)*

*Isaiah 53 TLB "But, oh, how few believe it! Who will listen? To whom will God reveal **his saving power**? In God's eyes, he was like a tender green shoot, sprouting from a root in dry and sterile ground. But **in our eyes, there was no attractiveness at all, nothing to make us want him**. **We despised him and rejected him**—a man of sorrows, acquainted with bitterest grief. We turned our backs on him and looked the other way when he went by. **He was despised, and we didn't care**.*

*Yet it was **our grief he bore, our sorrows that weighed him down**. And we thought his troubles were a punishment from God, for his own sins! But **he was wounded and bruised for our sins. He was beaten that we might have peace; he was lashed—and we were healed!** We—every one of us—have strayed away like sheep! **We, who left God's paths to follow** *__our own. Yet God laid on him the guilt and sins of every one of us!__*

He was oppressed and he was afflicted, yet he never said a word. He was brought as a lamb to the slaughter; and as a sheep before her shearers is silent, so he stood silent before the ones condemning him. From prison and trial they led him away to his death. ***But who among the people of that day realized it was*** *__their__* ***sins that he was dying for—*** *__that he was suffering their punishment?__* *He was buried like a criminal, but in a rich man's grave; but he had done no wrong and had never spoken an evil word.*

But it was the Lord's good plan to bruise him and fill him with grief. However, when his soul has been made an offering for sin, then he shall have a multitude of children, many heirs. He shall live again, and God's program shall prosper in his hands. And when he sees all that is accomplished by the anguish of his soul, he shall be satisfied; and ***because of what he has experienced, my righteous Servant shall make many to be counted righteous before God, for he shall bear all their sins***. *Therefore, I will give him the honours of one who is mighty and great because he has poured out his soul unto death.* ***He was counted as a sinner, and he bore the sins of many, and he pled with God for sinners***." *(emphasis added by me)*

Colossians 2:15 NLT "In this way, he disarmed the spiritual rulers and authorities. He shamed them publicly by his victory over them on the cross."

He desires for us to love Him with our all and serve Him wholeheartedly because He knows that is what our souls need. This might not make sense now, however, the reason why our souls need

Him it's because our souls are thirsting daily for the One that breathed life into us.

When God created us, He breathed life into us. The breath in our lungs came from God and because of that, your soul longs for Him even though you don't realise it or think that you don't need Him. Think about it!? Why are people so focused on being liked, or accepted, or even seek for relationships?? Why do we long for connections with people in the first place if we are just a bunch of atoms combined? Think about it?!

YOU LONG FOR A CONNECTION BECAUSE YOU WERE CREATED TO BE CONNECTED.

Why do we get upset and disappointed when people fail us, betray us, or leave us…? Because we seek a kind of love, a connection that will never break because that is what we need, because we know we cannot do life on our own. We are dependent on something that this world and no man (that is no human being) can offer,

UNCONDITIONAL LOVE!

If the Father was willing to send His Son to die for us and grant us eternal life, what won't He give us? What will He keep from us? God is not trying to keep you all to Himself and do nothing else, He wants you to enjoy the beauties He created on Earth. He ultimately wants you to find your satisfaction in Him, to enjoy His presence.

I am not talking about materialistic blessings. Of course, God gives materialistic blessings, for gold and silver are His and He created everything we see!

However, I am talking about spiritual blessings; salvation, freedom from sin, peace, joy, rest, etc. Things that only His presence can offer but that we seek in the world. Since it can't offer it to us, we jump from place to place, person to person, attempt after attempt trying to fill that void which is crying out loud from within us.

Nonetheless, since it cannot be found where we are searching, some people just end up giving up thinking that their lives are worth nothing. Every single droplet of Jesus' blood was shed for every one of us, so no one's life is worth nothing, our exitance matters, even if it doesn't to those around you it matters to God, and His approval is the one that matters.

> *Psalm 139:13-14 ESV " For you formed my inward parts; you knitted me together in my mother's womb. I praise you, for I am fearfully and wonderfully made. Wonderful are your works; my soul knows it very well."*

> *Psalm 27:10 NIV "Though my father and mother forsake me, the Lord will receive me."*

> *Romans 8:38-39 NLT "And I am convinced that **nothing can ever separate us from God's love**. Neither death nor life, neither angels nor demons, neither our fears for today nor our worries about tomorrow—not even the powers of hell can separate us from God's love. No power in the sky above or in the earth below—indeed, **nothing in all creation will ever be able to separate us from the love of God that is revealed in Christ Jesus our Lord**." (emphasis added by me)*

The Father's love for you was demonstrated at the cross, but also every time Jesus calls out sin in your life. Jesus is the Father's tangible expression of His love for us and it was shown at the cross where **mercy** and **justice** met. It is not just about saying yes to everything that you want it is also about saying no.

Love protects; indifference kills.

8

CONSEQUENCES OF A LIFE SEPARATED FROM CHRIST

Firstly, I want to begin with a summary of what this chapter will be about. There is a destination awaiting all of us (Romans 3:23). However, God made a way through Jesus (Hebrews 10:19-20, John 14:6) to escape the condemnation we are all heading towards, for those who reject THE ONLY WAY, they suffer the consequences of their sin (Matthew 21:44, Romans 6:23) <u>since they have no other means by which to be forgiven and freed from sin's slavery and penalty apart from Jesus' sacrifice</u> (Hebrews 10:26).

I want to begin with a story Jesus spoke of in Matthew 22 called the parable of the wedding dinner.

Matthew 22: 1-14 ESV "And again, Jesus spoke to them in parables, saying, "The kingdom of heaven may be compared to a king who gave a wedding feast for his son, and sent his servants to call those who were invited to the wedding feast, but they would not come. Again he sent other servants, saying, 'Tell those who are invited, "See, I have prepared my dinner, my oxen and my fat calves have been slaughtered, and everything is ready. Come to the wedding feast." ' But they paid no attention and went off, one to his farm, another to his business, while the rest seized his servants, treated them shamefully, and killed them.

The king was angry, and he sent his troops and destroyed those murderers and burned their city. Then he said to his servants, 'The wedding feast is ready, but those invited were not worthy. Go therefore to the main roads and invite to the wedding feast as many as you find.' And those servants went out into the roads and gathered all whom they found, both bad and good. So the wedding hall was filled with guests.

*"But when the king came in to look at the guests, he saw there a man who **had no wedding garment**. And he said to him, '**Friend, <u>how did you get in here without a wedding garment?</u>**' And he was speechless. Then the king said to the attendants, 'Bind him hand and foot and cast him into the **outer darkness**. In that place there will be **weeping and gnashing of teeth**.' <u>**For many are called, but few are chosen**</u>." (emphasis added by me)*

In this passage, we see two types of invitations. The first invitation invited them to the feast, the second invitation was to inform them that everything was ready.

In this story the master (the Father) invited people, but they refused to go because they preferred to go to their farms and their businesses. The Father has a wedding feast prepared in heaven, the Marriage of the Lamb (lamb referring to Jesus, John 1:29).

The marriage of the Lamb is the union of Jesus and His bride, the church. That is all Christians. It is not to be taken literally, it refers to the perfect union between Jesus and Christians in a spiritual sense. The complexity of the matter is far too great for our human, finite minds. However, I wanted to address it, so you had a rough idea of its meaning.

There is something key to notice in this story; the master invited. However, it was the guests that needed to take the action of accepting the invitation. They were aware of the master's invitation; He had reached out to them, but they did not respond.

Only by God's grace can we come to him (John 6:44). He draws us to Himself because, on our own, we would never seek God (Romans 3:10-18). It was the master who sent the invitations in the first place. However, we must respond to His invitation, His 'drawing' us.

From the passage, we can see how people aware of the feast rejected the invitation. Whereas others also knew about it but accepted the invitation.

The guests needed to wear specific clothing.

*Isaiah 61:10 NASB "I will rejoice greatly in the Lord, my soul will be joyful in my God; for **He has clothed me with garments of salvation, He has wrapped me with a robe of righteousness**, as a groom puts on a turban, and as a bride adorns herself with her jewels."*

This is the clothing people <u>receive</u> when they repent and put their faith in Jesus as Lord and Saviour; <u>the garments of salvation and a robe of righteousness</u>. Their sinfulness is exchanged for Jesus' righteousness, and now the Father does not see their sins but His Son's righteousness (Hebrews 8:12, Isaiah 43:25, Psalms 32:1).

CHRIST IS THE ONE WHO PROVIDES THE GARMENT AND THE ROBE. CHRIST IS OUR RIGHTEOUSNESS.

In 2 Corinthians 6 God warns us to not take His grace for granted,

2 Corinthians 6:1-2 NASB "And working together with Him, we also urge you not to receive the grace of God in vain— for He says, "At a favourable time I listened to you, and on a day of salvation I helped you." Behold, now is "a favourable time," behold, now is "a day of salvation."

Romans 2:4 NASB "Or do you think lightly of the riches of His kindness and restraint and patience, not knowing that the kindness of God leads you to repentance."

*2 Corinthians 5:18-21 NLT "[18] And **all of this is a gift from God**, who brought us back to himself **through Christ**. And*

*God has given us this task of reconciling people to him. [19]For God was in Christ, reconciling the world to himself, no longer counting people's sins against them. And he gave us this wonderful message of reconciliation. [20]So we are Christ's ambassadors; God is making his appeal through us. **We speak for Christ when we plead, "Come back to God!"** [21]For God made Christ, who never sinned, to be the offering for our sin, so that we could be made right with God through Christ." (emphasis added by me)*

I want to emphasize verse 21 because it's the most complex. This verse aims to highlight that <u>there is no greater reason for reconciliation with God other than the suffering and death of Jesus Christ</u>. No other argument will cause such a deep necessity to run towards the holy God for reconciliation.

On the cross, God treated Jesus as if He were a sinner (even though He wasn't guilty of any sin; John 18:38, Luke 23:22) and therefore poured on Him what is deserving of sinners, God's wrath. God poured on Jesus the wrath we deserved and treated Him instead as the sinner (as He was the sacrifice for our sins) and imputed Jesus's righteousness to us, treating those who place their faith in Jesus as righteous.

In the cross, a substitution occurred. Our sins were placed upon Him, and He was treated the way we should have been treated. He bore the punishment that we should of bore.

OUR SINS WERE SUBSTITUTED FOR HIS RIGHTEOUSNESS.

Jesus' sufferings are the greatest argument that causes people to see their necessity of the Savior because His sufferings were an illustration/manifestation of God's hatred for sin, its evil nature, and its consequences. <u>To know that you and I deserved that and instead were shown grace… nothing is more powerful than the cross.</u>

IF THE CROSS DOESN'T LEAD YOU TO YOUR KNEES, NOTHING IN THIS WORLD WILL.

*John 3:16-21 ESV "For God so loved the world, that he gave his only Son, that whoever believes in him should not **perish** but have **eternal life**. For God did not send his Son into the world to condemn the world, but in order that the world might be saved through him. Whoever believes in him is not condemned, but whoever does not believe is **condemned** already, because he has not believed in the name of the only Son of God. And this is the judgment: the light has come into the world, and people loved the darkness rather than the light because their works were evil. For everyone who does wicked things hates the light and does not come to the light, lest his works should be exposed. But whoever does what is true comes to the light, so that it may be clearly seen that his works have been carried out in God." (emphasis added by me)*

Perish means absolute destruction. That is a life of breaking God's law, far from His purpose for your life, and a life without what makes it truly worthwhile, Jesus.

When someone commits a crime, they are separated from society and everyday life, to be brought to prison and punished for their crimes. Similarly, it is in the spiritual. We are guilty of breaking God's law (1 John 3:4). Therefore, we deserve to go to 'prison'; however, the consequences of transgressions against a holy, eternal God can only be eternal since He is eternal, and so is our soul.

Psalm 119:142 NLT "Your <u>justice</u> is <u>eternal</u> [...]" (emphasis added by me)

So, this means that those who do not respond to the invitation of salvation and eternal life found only in Jesus remain in this state of condemnation.

1 John 3:23 NLT "and this is his commandment, that we believe in the name of his Son Jesus Christ and love one another, just as he has commanded us."

To believe Jesus Christ is to believe the gospel of Jesus, that is that He is the Son of God, that He came to die for our sins and rose from the dead, and that we are saved by placing our faith in His complete and sufficient sacrifice.

1 Corinthians 15:3-5 NIV "For what I received I passed on to you as of first importance: that Christ died for our sins according to the Scriptures, that he was buried, that he was raised on the third day according to the Scriptures, and that he appeared to Cephas, and then to the Twelve."

Disbelief in the gospel of Jesus is in itself breaking God's command for us.

John 16:9 NLT "The world's sin is that it refuses to believe in me."

However, notice what the passage says, "they have already been condemned."

In the same way, we don't have to go to heaven to experience eternal life (since we get a glimpse of it through encounters with God; Romans 8:23), similarly those who are condemned experience that already, that is, through a life separated from God. A life of searching for what can satisfy yet still feeling empty, running from person to person, place to place without finding the meaning of life or even having it all (materialistically speaking), yet your soul is still in need of something greater.

*1 John 5:11-12 ESV "And this is the testimony, that **God gave us eternal life, and this life is in his Son.** Whoever has the Son has life; **whoever does not have the Son of God does not have life**." (emphasis added by me)*

I want to go back to the passage in John 3 and talk about what it means for the "light came to the world" and when it talks about *"people preferred the darkness."*

According to John 8:12, the light is Jesus. Darkness is commonly associated with sin in the bible. Therefore, by saying that Jesus came into the world, yet the people preferred the darkness, is saying that Jesus came to give something better (SALVATION), however, people preferred to indulge in *"[...] physical pleasure, a craving for everything we see and pride in our achievements and possessions."* (1 John 2:16 NLT). This speaks of the sinful condition in which we are all born.

David describes himself as "shaped in iniquity" (Psalm 51:5 KJ21). In this Psalm, he was talking about the sin he had committed and asking God for forgiveness. However, he could only describe the immensity of the sin committed and the natural inclination towards sin as being "shaped in iniquity."

He committed adultery and planned to 'accidentally' murder the husband of the woman with whom he had committed adultery.

It is important to establish an essential truth here; this verse does not affirm that this was done by divine power, that is, being inclined towards evil and sin. In no manner was God the director nor the influence of such evil acts of his, but man is.

I bring up David's statement of "shaped in iniquity" because John 3 said that people rejected the light because they preferred the darkness. That is, we are naturally inclined towards sin.

Referring to the parable of the feast, people were aware of the master's invitation but still they rejected it because they were too busy seeking perishable treasures rather than finding the real treasure, Jesus.

Matthew 13:44 NASB "The kingdom of heaven is like a treasure hidden in the field, which a man found and hid again; and from joy over it he goes and sells everything that he has and buys that field."

Isn't it bizarre? The one who owns all glory and power and silver and gold (Philippians 2:6-11, Haggai 2:8) left it all to come and offer us salvation, yet we, who are poor, wretched and needy… forsake the real treasure for perishable ones?

Now, I need you to carefully think and examine yourself with what I will talk about now. I want you to ask yourself, AM I A GOOD PERSON? If so, why?

To check if you are right or not, we will go through the list of the ten commandments given by God, which, if you have not broken, means that you have not sinned (as sin is the transgression of God's law according to 1 John 3:4) and you are innocent before God, which the Bible says no one is; 1 John 1:10 NLT *"If we claim we have not sinned, we are calling God a liar and showing that his word has no place in our hearts."* If, as you self-examine, you find yourself guilty of just one, you are already guilty of them all before the eyes of God (James 2:10).

*Exodus 20:1-17 NLT "I am the Lord your God, who rescued you from the land of Egypt, the place of your slavery. **You must not have any other god but me.***

You must not make for yourself an idol of any kind or an image of anything in the heavens or on the earth or in the sea. You must not bow down to them or worship them [...]

You must not misuse the name of the Lord your God [...]

Remember to observe the Sabbath day by keeping it holy. You have six days each week for your ordinary work, but the seventh day is a Sabbath day of rest dedicated to the Lord your God [...]

Honour your father and mother [...] You must not murder. You must not commit adultery. You must not

steal. You must not testify falsely against your neighbour. You must not covet [...]" (emphasis added by me)

As I ask you these questions, I need you to self-examine and answer them in your head or with whoever is beside you as you read this.

1. First, have you ever used the name of God in vain? That is to express disgust.

2. Second, have you ever stolen anything, even if it's small? If so, what do you call someone who steals…?

3. Third, have you ever looked at a man (if who is reading this is a woman) or at a woman (if who is reading this is a man) and had lustful thoughts in your mind? If so, what is a person who looks at someone with lustful desires….?

(I'll give you a hint for this one, it might not be so quick to see, check on your phone or your bible at home if you have one Matthew 5:28.)

Having answered only those three questions, ask yourself, am I guilty or innocent? Have I broken at least one, if not all, of the commandments, or have I not?

What eternal destiny awaits me according to my answer…? Heaven or hell?

Now, to see what I mean by this "test", I'll do it myself so you can see what I mean. [This 'test' is seen in the ministry of Living Waters by Ray Comfort].

First, I have used God's name in vain.

Second, have I stolen? Sadly, yes, I have. That makes me a THIEF. Even if it's something tiny, it is still considered stealing…!

Third, I have looked at men and had lustful thoughts… which means I am an adulterer at heart.

According to those three answers and the ten commandments, I have at least broken three of the ten commandments. Therefore, being honest with myself, I must say that before the eyes of God, I would be guilty, so my eternal destination would be hell.

Now, why am I asking you to do this? Because it is important that you understand that no one that is in hell was put there forced by God, but they are deserving of God's wrath because they are 'GUILTY,' and God's wrath is essentially the expression of hatred He has towards sin.

According to the Bible, we are ALL deserving of hell since no one is good but God (Mark 10:18, Note: when Jesus responds why you call me good only God is, He is saying that the person that called Him good was recognizing that He is God since only God is good, and the person called Jesus good).

Romans 3:11-12 ESV "No one understands; no one seeks for God. All have turned aside; together they have become worthless; no one does good, not even one."

Romans 3:23 NLT "For <u>everyone has sinned</u>; we all fall short of <u>God's glorious standard</u>." (emphasis added by me)

Ecclesiastes 7:20 NASB1995 "Indeed, <u>there is not a righteous man on earth who continually does good and who never sins</u>." (emphasis added by me)

Psalm 14:1, 3 NASB1995 "The fool has said in his heart, "There is no God." They are corrupt, they have committed abominable deeds; <u>there is no one who does good</u>"/ "<u>They have all turned aside</u>, together they have become corrupt; There is <u>no one who does good</u>, not even one." (emphasis added by me)

Now, you may ask why God puts people in hell. And the answer is that we were already on our way there because of our sins! What He did was intervene and offer us a way out! However, if we reject the Only way out, then there's nothing that can save you.

*Acts 4:11- NLT "For Jesus is the one referred to in the Scriptures, where it says, 'The stone that you builders rejected has now become the cornerstone. **"There is salvation in no one else! God has given no other name under heaven by which we must be saved."** (emphasis added by me)*

This is important for me to talk to you about because there is a destiny for those who reject God's invitation to eternal life through Jesus Christ's sacrifice.

Why should there be a punishment at all? As clearly explained in this chapter, we have all sinned against a holy and just God, and we have done this by breaking His law, which makes us guilty in His sight.

Why doesn't He 'just' forgive if He is good? Well, God is a hundred percent Good but He is also a hundred percent Holy and Just. To put it in simpler terms, let me give you an analogy; say someone commits a crime (even if it's just one). Would a good judge just let him go because the criminal says well, I have done good things so wouldn't that counterbalance my crimes? We would expect a good and just judge to punish this individual irrespective of whether he has done good deeds before the crimes.

Similarly, God is good, just and holy and precisely because that's His nature is the reason why He cannot, by any means, leave sin unpunished.

Why an eternal punishment? Isn't that harsh and unloving? Since sin is committed against an Eternal God, it only makes sense for the punishment to be eternal; plus, that also gives us an insight into how monstrous sin is, that it requires an eternal punishment. Also, let's use this analogy. If you disrespect your mum, the punishment will be less severe than disrespecting a police officer. If we disrespect the president, the punishment would be more severe than disrespecting a police officer. So my point is that the higher in rank you go, the more severe the punishment becomes. So if we sin against a Holy, Eternal, All-powerful God, it makes sense that the punishment is the most severe.

It is important to understand that it is not a matter of 'do things my way or else'… We are all on our way to hell, our inclinations are corrupted by sin, and you may wonder, how is Adam's sin applied to me? I haven't done anything… Well, if we were given the choice of either a) repenting of our sins and placing our faith in Christ Jesus or b) wealth, fame, parties, sex… whatever it is that you enjoy the most…? I am pretty confident that we would choose whatever makes us feel good. That is a life with no awareness (or at least refusing to believe so) of having to give God an account for our life.

If you don't believe me, ask yourself; do I prefer that relationship in which I can indulge in sexual sin with no remorse of being judged by God or going to that party where all my friends will go and would make me feel more popular or more included… or do I prefer repenting from my sins and turning to God? We both know that the first choice is the most appealing one to the eyes.

God warns us so much and commands us to repent and turn to Him repeatedly to escape the destination we are heading to, hell. You may think that if He is God, why doesn't He make us believe? Or why does He give us the potential to sin? Well, if He forced you to love Him when He created you, it wouldn't be love because you were designed to do it. You would be a robot, not a human being.

Joel 2:13 NLT "[…] Return to the. Lord your God, <u>for he is merciful and compassionate, slow to get angry and filled with unfailing love</u>. He is eager to relent and not punish." (emphasis added by me)

2 Peter 3:9 NLT "The Lord isn't really being slow about his promise, as some people think. No, <u>he is being patient for your sake. He does not want anyone to be destroyed, but wants everyone to repent</u>." (emphasis added by me).

Matthew 4:17 NLT "From then on Jesus began to preach. "<u>Repent of your sins and turn to God</u>, for the Kingdom of Heaven is near" (emphasis added by me).

Ezekiel 18:32 NLT "<u>I don't want you to die, says the Sovereign Lord. Turn back and live!</u>" (emphasis added by me)

Acts 17:30-31 NLT "God overlooked people's ignorance about these things in earlier times, but now <u>he commands everyone everywhere to repent of their sins and turn to him. For he has set a day for judging the world with justice</u> by the man he has appointed, and he proved to everyone who this is by raising him from the dead." (emphasis added by me)

Ezekiel 33:10 NLT "Son of man, give the people of Israel this message: You are saying 'Our sins are heavy upon us; we are wasting away! How can we survive?." Only God's forgiveness can save us. God's desire is not to condemn us, but to save us.

John 12:47 NLT "I will not judge those who hear me but don't obey me, for <u>I have come to save the world and not to judge it</u>." (emphasis added by me)

[To avoid a misinterpretation of this verse, I'll explain it. When Jesus first came, He came to save us, that is, to show us the way to salvation and to reveal the Father to us. However, Jesus' second coming will only involve judgment, the judgement of the wicked. That is why He said He doesn't judge those who hear but don't obey, referring to the fact that He won't do it during His first appearance.]

It is essential to see that even though His second coming involves judgment, He first clarified the way to be saved, and He offered salvation before performing judgment on those who didn't and still don't believe. That is the evidence that His greatest desire is for us to believe and therefore have eternal life (John 3:36). However, not all will, so judgment must occur because sin cannot go unpunished.

Ezekiel 33:11 NLT "As surely as I live, says the Sovereign Lord, I take no pleasure in the death of wicked people. <u>I only want them to turn from their wicked ways so they can live</u>. Turn! Turn from your wickedness [...] Why should you die?" (emphasis added by me)

Ezekiel 18:25-29 ESV "Yet you say, 'The way of the Lord is not just.' Hear now, O house of Israel: Is my way not just? Is it not your ways that are not just? When a righteous person turns away from his righteousness and does injustice, he shall die for it; for the injustice that he has done he shall die. Again, when a wicked person turns away from the wickedness he has committed and does what is just and right, he shall save his life. Because <u>he considered and turned away from all the transgressions</u> he had committed, he shall surely live; he shall not die. Yet the house of Israel says, 'The way of the Lord is not just.' O house of Israel, are my ways not just? Is it not your ways that are not just?" (emphasis added by me)

This passage said something key: *"the wicked person considered and turned away from his transgressions."* Unless we are aware of our sin (realizing we are guilty before the eyes of God; John 16:7-8) and of our inability to save ourselves, we won't see the need for the Savior.

In Luke 16, Jesus tells the story of a rich man and a poor man called Lazarus.

Luke 16:19-31 NASB "Now there was a rich man, and he habitually dressed in purple and fine linen, enjoying himself in splendour every day. And a poor man named Lazarus was laid at his gate, covered with sores, and longing to be fed from the scraps which fell from the rich man's table; not only that, the dogs also were coming and licking his sores. Now it happened that the poor man died and was carried away by the angels to Abraham's arms; and the rich man also died and was buried. (emphasis added by me)

And in Hades he raised his eyes, <u>being in torment</u>, and saw Abraham far away and Lazarus in his arms. And he cried out and said, 'Father Abraham, have mercy on me and send Lazarus, so that he may dip the tip of his finger in water and cool off my tongue, for <u>I am in agony in this flame</u>' But Abraham said, 'Child, remember that during your life you received your good things, and likewise Lazarus bad things; but now he is being comforted here, and <u>you are in agony</u>.

And besides all this, between us and you a great chasm has been set, so that those who want to go over from here to you will not be able, nor will any people cross over from there to us.' And he said, 'Then I request of you, father, that you send him to my father's house— for I have five brothers— <u>in order that he may warn them, so that they will not come to this place of torment as well</u>.' But Abraham said, 'They have Moses and the Prophets; let them hear them.' But he said, 'No, father Abraham, but if someone goes to them from the dead, they will repent!' But he said to him, 'If they do not listen to Moses and the Prophets, they will not be persuaded even if someone rises from the dead.'" (emphasis added by me)

Hades can have different meanings depending on the context in which it is written, but it's always related to death, where spirits go.

This passage it's referring specifically to the place where wicked spirits go.

First, let me clarify the meaning of wicked. A wicked person lives breaking God's law and is not repentant or sorrowful.

From the description of the rich man, it is evident that it is a place of punishment. It is crucial to notice the man's persistence in sending a sign to his brothers to make them aware "of this place of torment." From the Bible, it is clear that hell is not comfortable. It is a place of torment, agony, and flames. This already proves any other view of hell as a place of "rest" or absent from judgment and pain to be false.

As unpopular as this topic is, it must be taught. Otherwise, people will only be partially aware of their spiritual condition, and above your comfort, I care more about your soul and its eternal destiny.

Since it took God to come as a man to die for us, save us, and warn us from this place, imagine the severity of this place.

Philippians 2:5-9 NLT "You must have the same attitude that Christ Jesus had. Though he was God, he did not think of equality with God as something to cling to. Instead, he gave up his divine privilege; he took the humble position of a slave and was born as a human being. When he appeared in human form, he humbled himself in obedience to God and died a criminal's death on a cross. Therefore, God elevated him to the place of highest honour and gave him the name above all other names."

Hell is described as follows according to the Bible:

- "Eternal fire, never-ending" (Matthew 25:41, 3:12 NLT).

- "Shame and everlasting disgrace" (Daniel 12:2 NLT).

- "Where the maggots never die and the fire never goes out" (Mark 9:44-48 NLT).

- "In torment" (Luke 16:23-24 NLT).

- "Eternal destruction" (2 Thessalonians 1:8-9 NLT).

- "Eternal punishment" (Matthew 25:46 NLT).

- "Indignation, wrath, tribulation and anguish" (Romans 2:8-9 NKJV).

- "Eternal fire, blackest darkness" (Jude 7,13 NLT).

I know this is a difficult topic, but because God loves you, He must warn you of your sin.

Ezekiel 18:23 NLT "Do you think that I like to see wicked people die? says the Sovereign Lord. Of course not! I want them to turn from their wicked ways and live."

9

REPENTANCE

The Bible is very clear about how to be saved.

John 3:36 NLT "And anyone who <u>believes</u> in God's Son has eternal life. Anyone who doesn't obey the Son will never experience eternal life but remains under God's angry judgment." (emphasis added by me)

1 John 3:23 NLT "And this is his commandment, that we <u>believe</u> in the name of his Son Jesus Christ and love one another, just as he has commanded us." (emphasis added by me)

John 3:16 NLT "For this is how God loved the world: He gave his one and only Son, so that everyone who <u>believes</u> in him will not perish but have eternal life." (emphasis added by me)

Acts 20:21 ESV "testifying both to Jews and to Greeks of <u>repentance toward God</u> and of <u>faith in our Lord Jesus Christ</u>." (emphasis added by me)

It is not complicated to see that the Bible clearly states that faith is what grants us eternal life. Faith that Jesus is the Son of God, that He died for our sins (suffered the wrath that we should have suffered for our sins) and was raised from the dead.

It is important to notice something when it says Jesus is the Son of God. It is essential to understand that Jesus carried God the Father's essence (Hebrews 1:3). It doesn't mean that God and Jesus are separated; God is three persons but one being (triune God). Like us, body, soul and spirit, yet they make one being, you.

However, going back to the verses. The Bible tells us in Ephesians 2:8-9 that <u>we are saved by grace</u>, not because of anything we may have done, so no one shall boast. Therefore, <u>there is no way we can work our way to heaven</u> because we are corrupted by sin, so any effort to earn our way to heaven is counted as filthy rags, according to Isaiah 64:6.

It is crucial to be aware of one's sins (the Holy Spirit convicts us of sin) to have faith in Jesus; otherwise, what is the need? One must acknowledge their sin, that is, recognise that we have sinned against God and recognise our need for His forgiveness (which cannot be earned; it is granted by grace).

Repentance can be visualised in Psalm 119:

Psalm 119:59 CSB "I thought about my ways and <u>turned</u> my steps back to your decrees." (emphasis added by me)

Essentially, repentance is a change of mind <u>regarding sin and Jesus</u>. We are usually all faced towards sin (comfortable in our sin) while we turn our back on God (in rebellion). Unless our view on sin changes, we cannot place our faith in Jesus Christ as Saviour because we won't see the need to do so.

Whether you were unaware of how detestable sin is to God or whether you acknowledge it yet ignore it, there's still a need for a change of mind regarding sin and Jesus. Repentance is when we once faced sin and turned our back on God, we now turn our back on sin and turn to God. We face sin because we reject Christ; when we give our back to sin, we recognize Christ as our Saviour.

REPENTANCE IS AN ATTITUDE OF HEART THAT NO LONGER DELIGHTS IN SIN IN LIGHT OF JESUS' SACRIFICE.

The Holy Spirit is the one who convicts us of our sins. There is absolutely nothing we bring to our salvation. Conviction is the work of the Holy Spirit. The way to heaven was taken care of by Jesus on the cross; growing to be more Christ-like, once saved, is by the work of the Holy Spirit… as you can see, we do not contribute to our salvation.

IT IS A GIFT!

However, it must not be taken lightly because it's a gift.

Hebrew 2:1-3 ESV "Therefore we must pay much closer attention to what we have heard, lest we drift away from it. For since the message declared by angels proved to be reliable, and every transgression or disobedience received a just retribution, <u>how shall we escape if we neglect such a great salvation?</u> It was declared at first by the Lord, and it was attested to us by those who heard." (emphasis added by me)

As we have seen in the previous chapter, it has terrible consequences to reject this gift. So, it is simple; it only takes faith.

Saving faith brings forth fruits of repentance which John the Baptist mentioned in Matthew 3:8 NLT *"Prove by the way you live that you have repented of your sins and turned to God."*

James later says that faith without works is dead.

James 2:14-24 NLT "What good is it, dear brothers and sisters, if you say you have faith but don't show it by your actions? Can that kind of faith save anyone? Suppose you see a brother or sister who has no food or clothing, and you say, "Good-bye and have a good day; stay warm and eat well"—but then you don't give that person any food or clothing. What good does that do? So you see, faith by itself isn't enough. Unless it produces good deeds, it is dead and useless.

Now someone may argue, "Some people have faith; others have good deeds." But I say, "How can you show me your faith if you don't have good deeds? I will show you my faith by my good deeds." You say you have faith, for you believe that there is one God. Good for you! Even the demons believe this, and they tremble in terror. How foolish! Can't you see that faith without good deeds is useless?

Don't you remember that our ancestor Abraham was <u>shown to be right with God by his actions</u> when he offered his son Isaac on the altar? You see, <u>his faith and his actions worked together</u>. His actions made his faith complete. And so it happened just as the Scriptures say: "Abraham believed God, and God counted him as righteous because of his faith." He was even called the friend of God. So you see, we are shown to be right with God by what we do, not by faith alone." (emphasis added by me)

Faith alone saves us, but works are the evidence that we have been saved. Works come as a result of a changed heart which now delights in Jesus, sees Him as precious and delights in living for Him.

Matthew 14:44-46 ESV "The kingdom of heaven is like <u>treasure</u> hidden in a field, which a man found and covered up. Then in his joy he goes and sells all that he has and buys that field. "Again, the kingdom of heaven is like a merchant in search of fine pearls, who, on finding <u>one pearl of great value</u>, went and sold all that he had and bought it"

Jesus is that treasure and that pearl of great value. Our works come about as a response to the Holy Spirit's work in us and our following of His directions. If we have been saved, Jesus will become precious to us:

1 Peter 2:6-8 ESV "For it stands in Scripture: "Behold, I am laying in Zion a stone, a cornerstone chosen and precious, and whoever believes in him will not be put to shame." So the honor is for you who believe, but for those who do not believe, "The stone that the builders rejected has become the cornerstone," and "A stone of stumbling, and a rock of offense."

Jesus is this cornerstone, chosen by God and precious to us, but for those who reject Him, He is an offense to them. Therefore, if He has become precious to us, how could we live the same way we used to? How could we delight in the things He died for?

1 Corinthians 6:9-11 ESV "Or do you not know that the unrighteous will not inherit the kingdom of God? Do not be deceived: neither the sexually immoral, nor idolaters, nor adulterers, nor men who practice homosexuality, nor thieves, nor the greedy, nor drunkards, nor revilers, nor swindlers will inherit the kingdom of God. And such were some of you. But you were washed, you were sanctified, you were justified in the name of the Lord Jesus Christ and by the Spirit of our God." (emphasis added by me)

1 Peter 1:14-16 ESV "As obedient children, do not be conformed to the passions of your former ignorance, but as he who called you is holy, you also be holy in all your conduct, since it is written, "You shall be holy, for I am holy." (emphasis added by me)

Romans 6:13 NLT "Do not let any part of your body become an instrument of evil to serve sin. Instead, give yourselves completely to God, for you were dead, but now you have new life. So use your whole body as an instrument to do what is right for the glory of God" (emphasis added by me).

Ephesians 2:10 ESV "For we are his workmanship, <u>created in Christ Jesus for good works</u>, which God prepared beforehand, <u>that we should walk in them</u>." (emphasis added by me)

Colossians 1:9-10 NLT "So we have not stopped praying for you since we first heard about you. We ask God to give you complete knowledge of his will and to give you spiritual wisdom and understanding. <u>Then the way you live will always honor and please the Lord</u>, and your lives will produce every kind of <u>good fruit</u>. All the while, you will grow as you learn to know God better and better." (emphasis added by me)

1 Thessalonians 4:1 ESV "Finally, then, brothers, we ask and urge you in the Lord Jesus, that as you received from us <u>how you ought to walk and to please God</u>, just as you are doing, <u>that you do so more and more</u>." (emphasis added by me)

2 Corinthians 5:9-10 ESV "So whether we are at home or away, <u>we make it our aim to please him</u>. For we must all appear before the judgment seat of Christ, so that each one may receive what is due for what <u>he has done in the body</u>, whether good or evil." (emphasis added by me)

As John 1:12 states that those who believe in Jesus as Lord and Saviour, are now children of God, and as children of God, now they live for Him.

One may read the verses in the book of James chapter 2 and think that he is saying that faith alone does not save, but that is not what he is saying. If you read the passage carefully, he discusses the <u>evidence of such faith</u>. Good deeds characterise saving faith because these bring glory to God (John 15:8). Good deeds show we love God (John 14:15) and also glorify God (Matthew 5:16).

"There must be true and deep conviction of sin. This the preacher must labor to produce, for where this is not felt, <u>the new birth</u> has not taken place"- Charles Spurgeon.

This new birth Spurgeon mentioned is in John 3:3, where Jesus told Nicodemus that no one could see the kingdom of God unless they are born again. Being born again describes what occurs when we place our faith in Jesus as Saviour. This commences such a dramatic change in our lives that a new nature is essentially granted by God in which we become new creatures (2 Corinthians 5:17), and in this new nature, in this new way of living, we can, by God's grace, live in a Christ-like manner (1 John 2:6).

Repentance is a change of mind. Moreover, it also implies regret for the sin committed and that sorrow will eventually lead to a desire to turn away from sin, to not delight in it (enabled by the Holy Spirit). It is a calling to a changed life, essentially.

In 2 Corinthians 5:17 NLT, the Bible speaks of the new creature and in Ephesians 4:22-24 NLT about the old man and the new man.

"This means that anyone who belongs to Christ has become a new person. The old life is gone; a new life has begun!"/ "throw off your old sinful nature and your former way of life, which is corrupted by lust and deception. Instead, let the Spirit renew your thoughts and attitudes. Put on your new nature, created to be like God—truly righteous and holy."

1 John 3:8-9 NLT "But when people keep on sinning, it shows that they belong to the devil, who has been sinning since the beginning. But the Son of God came to destroy the works of the devil. Those born into God's family do not <u>practice</u> sin [that is, their lives are not characterised by a life indulged in sin] because God's life is in them. So they can't keep on sinning because they are children of God."

(emphasis added by me). Note: I added brackets for clarification.

Those who are children of God do not delight in sin. <u>The apostle meant in this verse that the **gospel is not a license to sin**</u>. Not because God is gracious and merciful and because we are saved by faith can we do what we please.

1 Corinthians 6:12 NIV "I have the right to do anything," you say—but not everything is beneficial. "I have the right to do anything"—but I will not be mastered by anything." The Corinthians wanted to used their freedom in Christ as a license to sin. Paul does emphatically repeat that we are free in Christ, free from trying to earn our way to heaven, free from trying to earn our salvation by works. However, Paul doesn't mean that this freedom is to be used as a license to sin, or as a justification for their sinful lifestyle.

Romans 6:1-3, 6-7, 10-18 NLT "Well then, should we keep on sinning so that God can show us more and more of his wonderful grace? Of course not! Since we have <u>died to sin</u>, how can we continue to live in it? Or have you forgotten that when we were joined with Christ Jesus in baptism, we joined him in his death?/

"We know that <u>our old sinful selves were crucified with Christ so that sin might lose its power in our lives</u>. We are no longer slaves to sin. For when we died with Christ we were set free from the power of sin" /

"When he [Jesus] died, he died once to break the power of sin. But now that he lives, he lives for the glory of God. So you also should consider yourselves to be dead to the power of sin and alive to God through Christ Jesus.

Do not let sin control the way you live; do not give in to sinful desires. Do not let any part of your body become an instrument of evil to serve sin. Instead, give yourselves *completely to God, for you were dead, but now you have <u>new life</u>. So use your whole body as an instrument to do what is right for the glory of God. Sin is no longer your master, for you no longer live under the requirements of the law [meaning not seeking to be justified by keeping the law]. Instead, you live under the freedom of God's grace [which enables us to essentially not live to satisfy our sinful desires, but to live to please God].*

Well then, since God's grace has set us free from the law, does that mean we can go on sinning? Of course not! Don't you realise that you become the slave of whatever you choose to obey? You can be a slave to sin, which leads to death, or you can choose to obey God, which leads to righteous living. Thank God! Once, you were slaves of sin, but now you wholeheartedly obey this teaching we have given you. Now you are free from your slavery to sin, and you have become slaves to righteous living." (emphasis added by me). Note: I added the brackets to clarify.

The apostle Paul is tackling the suggestion of giving license to sin freely without remorse or regret. People may try to suggest that, since those who place their faith in Jesus are under grace (which provides forgiveness of sins, and we are no longer under the law, which requires complete obedience), they can go on sinning freely without feeling the obligation to live holy as He is holy (1 Peter 1:16). To which Paul responds <u>absolutely not</u> since when we place our faith in Jesus, we are crucifying our sinful desires (Galatians 5:24), now we are living for Him who saved us (2 Corinthians 5:15).

*Romans 10:9 NASB "That if you **confess** with your mouth Jesus as Lord, and **believe in your heart** that God raised Him from the dead, you will be **saved**." (emphasis added by me)*

*2 Peter 3:9 NLT "The Lord isn't really being slow about his promise, as some people think. No, **He is being patient for your sake**. He does not want anyone to be destroyed, but wants everyone **to repent**." (emphasis added by me)*

*Hebrews 2:3 NLT "So **what makes us think we can escape if we ignore this great salvation** that was first announced by the Lord Jesus himself and then delivered to us by those who heard him speak?" (emphasis added by me)*

*Joel 2:12-13 NIV "Even now," declares the Lord, "**return to me with all your heart, with fasting and weeping and mourning**." Rend your heart and not your garments. **Return to the Lord your God**, for he is gracious and compassionate, slow to anger and abounding in love, and he relents from sending calamity." (emphasis added by me)*

*2 Corinthians 5:20-21 NLT "So we are Christ's ambassadors; God is making his appeal through us. **We speak for Christ when we plead, "Come back to God!"** For God made Christ, who never sinned, to be the offering for our sin, so that we could be made right with God through Christ." (emphasis added by me)*

*Isaiah 55:6-7 NLT "**Seek the Lord while you can find him**. Call on him now while he is near. Let the wicked change their ways and banish the very thought of doing wrong. Let them turn to the Lord that he may have mercy on them. **Yes, turn to our God, for he will forgive generously**." (emphasis added by me)*

*2 Corinthians 6:1-2 NIV "As God's co-workers **we urge you not to receive God's grace in vain**. For he says, "In the* *time of my favour I heard you, and in the day of salvation I helped you." I tell you,* **now is the time of God's favour, now is the day of salvation.***" (emphasis added by me)*

All the glory to the one who called me to write this book. He is the author and the one who deserves all glory and praise for His abundant goodness poured unto us through the grace and mercy of our saviour, Jesus Christ!

For more information contact:

Monica Rosario Santos
C/O Advantage Books
info@advbooks.com

To purchase additional copies of this books visit our bookstore
at www.advbookstore.com

Orlando, Florida, USA
"we bring dreams to life"™
www.advbookstore.com